England in cameracolour
# Lake District

To the Cadwalladers
for being such wonderful people

Christmas 1982
Franklin Ishida

# England in cameracolour
# Lake District

Photographs by F. A. H. BLOEMENDAL

Text by GEOFFREY BEARD

LONDON

IAN ALLAN LTD

First published 1979

ISBN 0 7110 0922 8

Published by Ian Allan Ltd, Shepperton, Surrey,
and printed in Italy by
Graphische Betriebe Athesia, Bolzano

# Introduction

Since the late seventeenth century travellers in search of dramatic scenery have ventured into the Lake District, intent on recording, drawing and revelling in the natural wonders around them. Bounded on the west by the Irish Sea, on the east by the Pennines, and at the north by the Roman majesty of Hadrian's Wall and the Scottish border is an area in which is set a near unrivalled assemblage of expansive lakes, great mountains and deep lonely valleys. Spanning for the most part large areas of the former counties of Cumberland and Westmorland – now Cumbria – the whole extent has a dozen lakes, the loftiest mountains in England and is ribboned by some 30 rivers and innumerable streams or becks. With a long history in geological and human terms, set out in many ways, the special nature of the English Lakes is not easily grasped, even after several visits.

William Wordsworth, most celebrated of the 'Lake Poets' first compiled his fascinating *A Guide to the Lakes* in 1810 from the knowledge of long acquaintance. Of 'Mountains: Their Forms and Colours' he wrote that 'in the combinations they make, towering above each other, or lifting themselves in ridges like the waves of a tumultuous sea, and in the beauty and variety of their surfaces and colours, they are surpassed by none . . .' We might then start with a brief note on the *geology,* the basis of the landscape. In simple terms the Lake District was formed by movements of the earth's crust of old hard rocks, and the processes of erosion and weathering. About 400 million years ago the Borrowdale Volcanic Series were shot out from steaming sulphurous vents to overlay the older Skiddaw Slates in the northern Lake District with the Silurian slate beds being laid on top of them. These three make all the mountains and all the peaks. The Borrowdale rocks encompass the Coniston Fells for example and stand above the Silurian lowlands to form very dramatic contrasts. In addition later rocks intruded – the newer limestones and sandstones – to give interesting variations and colours. But it is the bold outlines and surface jointing of the Borrowdale Volcanics which dominate, 'perpetually changed by the clouds and vapours which float round them'. In a total thickness of some eight to twelve thousand feet there is also rich mineral wealth.

The final force in the formation and sculpturing of mountains and valleys was glacial action, scouring and scraping all before it over a million years. It intensified the cragginess on a bold scale, forming the great points of Scafell, Gable, Pillar, Great End, and the steep valley sides. Many of the high mountain tarns, or small lakes, are set in the corries worn out by glacial action. The soft rocks were ground to expose harder bands and rock steps, often now with dramatic waterfalls. The head of Great Langdale, and the Borrowdale valley show many traces of the effects of glaciation. It also gave to the Lakes themselves their particular character and this has been more recently emphasised by differences in vegetation – the wooded shores of Coniston and Derwentwater contrasted to the bare fells of Ennerdale Water and Crummock. A visitor also soon has to come to terms with the *climate,* the rain, the thunder, the ladders of sun-light piercing mist, and the high crisp blue skies, in a world of endless contrasts.

The Lake District lies between the latitude lines of 54° and 55°N but has the special characteristic of its mountains and its ocean-girded western shore-line to shape its climate. The precipitation of rain or snow increases rapidly as the clouds are borne towards the heads of the radiating valleys. It has been noted 'that five times as much rain falls in a small patch near Sprinkling Tarn beneath Great End' compared to Low Furness – some 185 inches on average. The expansion and cooling of the air stream as it rises towards and over the mountains results in wet areas, with a rapid diminution on the sheltered sides to the east. The damp Atlantic air is frequently unstable and no rain on the coast may well mean sharp cold showers in the mountain ranges. The glaciated fells can also, by their geological make-up, have wet peaty patches alongside a free-draining slope.

In spite of the many fluctuations in the rainfall levels in the Lake District the amount of sunshine compares favourably with points in similar latitudes, with an average at Keswick during June of 181 hours. Ambleside, several miles to the south, and surrounded by hills, records about 60 hours less across the year. The Lake District has a reputation for its heavy rainfall, and its extremes of rainfall and the persistence of low cloud is well known. It gave the watercolourists in the eighteenth and nineteenth centuries what they sought in contrasting scenery, and it often happens, as John Ruskin recorded on June 22, 1876 – 'it cleared suddenly, after raining all afternoon, at half-past eight to nine, into pure, natural weather, low rain-clouds on quite clear, green wet hills'. Ruskin was at his house of Brantwood, with its spectacular views from the east bank of Coniston Water, one of the smaller lakes.

The clouds often envelop the mountains – the highest in England, with the Scafell Pikes at 3,166ft commanding a prospect of the greater part of Cumberland. 'All the coast from St Bee's Head to Solway Firth, with the several bays and promontories, the Isle of Man, and a considerable portion of the southern part of Scotland' can be seen. When Mannix and Whelan compiled their 'History, Gazetteer and Directory' of Cumberland in 1847 they quoted from William Green on the 'value of prospects' from the mountains, and in particular Skiddaw:

'in beholding a country richly variegated with fields of corn, fit for the sickle, meadows, green as emerald, hills clad with purple heath, lakes, with winding shores and beautiful islands, rivers shining like silver as they shape their serpentine courses towards the Irish Sea, and in tracing the effects of light and shade upon mountains in every imaginable diversity of form'.

The hazy memory of school-days' geography, which often prompts the first visit to the Lake District, is to recall the name of Helvellyn. Situated on the east side of the Keswick and Ambleside road, opposite Thirlmere Lake, its western side smooth and convex shows the pre-glacial mountain shape, and snow may lie on its highest coves till June. H. H. Symonds who wrote one of the best guides to walking in the Lake District (supplanted perhaps by the internationally known guides by Alfred Wainwright) said 'catch Helvellyn on the right day and you have, I think, the best of all the views from the bigger fells; while the view from the intervening summit as you go near Blea Tarn is a splendid one, not only to north and west, but in front of you down on to the waters of Thirlmere'. The best way to Helvellyn is by Striding Edge, a steady rising walk increasing in interest throughout to·the summit 'where the whole of Cumberland lies westward before you in a shattering surprise'.

As for surface we can do no better than Wordsworth's basic description: 'the general surface of the mountains is turf, rendered rich and green by the moisture of the climate'. We need however to qualify his words with the more accurate observations made by the various authors in Pearsall and Penningtons' landscape history *The Lake District* (1973):

'on the grassy mountains of the central Lake District three broad zones can be distinguished: the lowest one in which bracken is now abundant, a middle one about 1,000 feet in which a poor mat grass (*Nardus stricta*) is prominent, and then the montane zone above about 2,000ft'.

6  At this higher level mosses and lichens gain a perilous hold in a short growing season,

with extreme exposure to wind and frost almost ever-present. Dorothy Wordsworth described in her Journal an excursion up Scaw Fell Pike on October 17, 1818:

'. . . our ascent to Scaw Fell Pike. There, not a blade of grass was to be seen – hardly a cushion of moss, and that was parched and brown; and only growing rarely between the huge blocks and stones which cover the summit, covered with near-dying lichens, which the clouds and dews nourish, and adorn with colours of the most vivid and exquisite beauty, and endless in variety'.

When Dr Ratcliffe compiled his *The Mountain Flora of Lakeland* in 1960 he noted some fifty-seven species on the north-east and east facing cliffs of Helvellyn at 2,600 to 2,800ft. While the mountain flora of the Lake District bears no comparison to that of the Alps, or the Scottish Highlands, there are areas richer in lime and other essential base nutrients to support an alpine vegetation. Faults in the Skiddaw Slate and Borrowdale Volcanic rocks are lime-rich, and inaccessible to grazing Herdwick sheep. The Lake District fells provide extensive pasture to the Herdwick and other mountain sheep. Also below about 1,000ft, and for some eight months of the year the slopes are covered with bracken, now spreading as cutting has ceased with the decline of the small farms. These fells also support four characteristic plants – the butterwort; yellow mountain saxifrage; Alpine lady's mantle and the Grass of Parnassus. There is also heather – to a much lesser extent than in Scotland – and bilberry on the acid moorlands.

In the meadowed valleys and the hill woods it is possible for the keen amateur with good binoculars to observe a great variety of wild life. Native red deer are a stirring sight in Martindale, at Ennerdale, on the Dalemain estate, west of Penrith, and in Grizedale forest. The red squirrel is appearing in greater numbers, although its natural enemy the stoat is never far away. The fox and badger are common, otters live in the lake margins and rivers, and the rare pine marten is found in Grizedale Forest, an area maintained with care, and with intelligent educational programmes arranged for visitors, by the Forestry Commission.

On the higher fells the buzzard soars, and while sheep carrion is its main food, it is still a stirring sight to see it gliding effortlessly on the strong wind currents. Wheatears and meadow pipits are commonly seen, and nest up to near 3,000ft, and there is always the kestrel, hovering and swooping with monotonous regularity, or the merlin, which nests on the heather fells, but preys on the smaller birds.

It is however to the lakes as well as the mountains that visitors have always thronged. Before the railway was extended to Windermere the old way of crossing the sands from Lancaster to Ulverston to enter the Lake District was a striking if dangerous route. Adam Walker who wrote *Remarks Made in a Tour from London to the Lakes* in 1792 said that on occasions he had crossed the sands 'when we were obliged to open the two doors of the chaise, and let the water run through'. With a guide leading through the shifting channels, it was the way John Wesley took in the 1740s, and it appealed to many for its sense of danger, and the vast desolate plains of sea and sand.

Wordsworth thought the form of a lake 'most perfect when, like Derwentwater, and some of the smaller lakes, it least resembles a river'. The early visitor, whether talented watercolourist like Francis Towne, or a careful writer and recorder like Thomas Pennant, was much assisted by many guide books by Dr John Brown, Thomas West and others. West's *Guide to the Lakes* contained very detailed instructions on the location of particular viewpoints which he called 'stations'. From these 'stations' many of the best views of the lakes could be obtained.

Windermere, the largest lake in England, above ten miles long, is crossed by a ferry a mile south of Bowness. On the approach from Bowness or Ambleside the lake bursts at once into sight and, dotted with many islets, is almost always busy with yachts, and boats   7 in propulsion. Away from its western shore at about two miles from the ferry is the small placid lake of Esthwaite Water with a fine swelling peninsula that extends into the water from its western shore. The mountains of Langdale, Grasmere and Rydal are seen to great advantage from the margin of this lake. Coniston Water in the Furness Fells, six miles in length, is also bounded by high mountains. West's 'first station' described Coniston from a little above the village of Nibthwaite, and Ruskin visited it when a boy of 11 in 1830, forty years before he settled at Brantwood on the eastern bank.

North-west of Ambleside, and in 'Wordsworth country' is the small Rydal Water, which empties into the river Rothay, which after a course of two miles, loses its waters in Windermere. The American writer Nathaniel Hawthorne visiting Rydal Water in July 1855 wrote that after leaving Ambleside he soon came 'to a sheet (or napkin, rather, than a sheet) of water, which the driver tells us is Rydal Lake! We had already heard that it was but three quarters of a mile long and one quarter broad . . . it certainly did look small, and I said, in my American scorn, that I could carry it away easily in a porringer, for it is nothing more than a grassy-bordered pool among the surrounding hills which ascend directly from its margin'.

A little to the west Grasmere Lake, about a mile in length, has a solitary green island set in its dark waters. Wordsworth lived with his sister Dorothy at Dove Cottage at Grasmere from the end of the eighteenth century. In the churchyard is Wordsworth's simple grave, but Matthew Arnold's verses on *The Death of Wordsworth, April 1850* remain the most poignant testimony:

*Goethe in Weimar sleeps, and Greece,*
*Long since, saw Byron's struggle cease.*
*But one such death remain'd to come;*
*The last poetic voice is dumb —*
*We stand today by Wordsworth's tomb.*

The road from Ambleside to Keswick, which skirts Grasmere village, also passes Thirlmere extended in the late nineteenth century by Manchester Corporation who send its water 90 miles to Manchester. It was a bitter struggle for the conservationists of the time and even as late as 1933 H. H. Symonds wrote of 'Thirlmere, bath of Mancunians'. The bracken-covered fell-sides were planted by the Manchester foresters with larch and beech to conserve the soil, with spruces and Douglas firs on the lower slopes. Fences excluded deer and sheep and this has allowed natural seeding of native trees.

Away to the north but just south of Keswick is perhaps one of the finest lakes, Derwentwater. Some three miles in length the shores are indented in a most agreeable way, and it appears to be entirely circled with mountains. Away to the south are the broken rocky mountains of Borrowdale, the smooth lines of Newlands on the west, or towering Skiddaw to the north. Its surface is broken by five islands, that of St Herbert's Island taking its name from a priest and confessor of the middle of the seventh century who made it his lonely home. At Friar's Crag on the eastern shore is the Ruskin monument, a bronze portrait medallion set in a block of slate and on it a sentence from his *Praeterita* — 'the first thing which I remember as an event in life was being taken by my nurse to the brow of Friar's Crag on Derwentwater'.

Three miles north-west of Keswick a range of lofty hills called Withrop Brows bound Bassenthwaite Lake, with majestic Skiddaw at the south-east. It has no islands but undulates between meadow-lands on its west bank and is skirted by the A66 road to the east. Between 1972 and 1976 the 'Friends of the Lake District' waged a long and intelligent campaign to stop the widening of the A66 with an embankment to carry the east-bound carriageway being built on piles out into the lake. They lost and irreparable harm was not only caused to a part of the National Park noted for its beauty, but to the rules which govern such areas as cogently set out in the Sandford Report. Transport problems have always loomed large in the Lake District and are increased by a too-ready acceptance of unrestrained movement of people and goods being given priority over environmental value.

Buttermere Lake, nine miles south of Bassenthwaite, is in a luxuriant valley encompassed by rocky mountains, except on the west. There is a green tone in the rocks common to the Volcanic Series, and best known is the green slate of Honister. Buttermere is better known however for the fell country around the lake. The valley provides good ridge walks on each flank, and the descents back to the village offer fine sweeping views, with variations in colour given by streaks of pink Ennerdale granite, and the reddish slate of Red Pike. Climbing to Red Pike from Scale Force, a long but manageable route brings sight of one of the dramatic features of the Lake District, 100 feet of sheer waterfall, good even in dry weather, and sinking into a tremendous chasm.

The Great Gable is also what H. H. Symonds called 'fair game from Buttermere'. Its hard volcanic rock attracted the intrepid mountaineers of the nineteenth century, keeping in trim for Alpine assaults. Here, on what A. H. Griffin has called 'The Roof of England' the National Trust was entrusted with guardianship, Great Gable and Great End being given to it by the Fell and Rock Climbing Club in 1923 as a War Memorial to its members killed in the 1914–18 War.

In western Cumbria there are lakes which are less frequented by visitors. Moving west from Buttermere and within a mile is Crummock Water. The best general views of it are from the rocky point on the eastern side, called the Hause. The celebrated waterfall of Scale Force is on the south-west side of Crummock. The pebbles on its shore are of Ennerdale granite and slate mixed, but it is a lovely shore much visited by too many besides pebble-gatherers. Two miles further west is Lowes Water where peace, woods and gentle fells are easier found near to the lake and in the green valleys leading to Mellbreak. The lofty mountains in the distance are ribboned by crystal springs which feed Ennerdale Water from which Whitehaven takes much water. But more is always wanted – for the nuclear power station at Windscale and for west coast industry and plans are in hand to raise the lake level by four feet.

'Ennerdale is a wild and dramatic place' Geoffrey Berry, Consultant Secretary of the Friends of the Lake District writes, where 'afforestation of the valley floor has not tamed its upper reaches, no building stands upon the lake shore, no motor road reaches beyond its entrance. It must be explored on foot. No other Lake District valley remains in such a state of primitive beauty'. To stand alone on its tree-girt shore, with Pillar Mountain in the background, and a great expanse of blue sky above; with the clouds sweeping great shadows as they roll across is to know at last the true Lake District.

Devoke Water, more properly a tarn, and six miles east of Ravenglass is connected to the River Esk, as is Wast Water. Here, within a few miles of the coast are surroundings of great majesty. On the south-east side of Wast Water are the famous Screes, a great profusion of loose stones, extending from near the summit of the surrounding mountains down into the water. By walking, rather than motoring by the road from the foot of the lake it is possible 'to appreciate the astounding rake of these screes, and their two miles of blackness, only at the pace of contemplation'.

Finally in a consideration of the lakes themselves we move east to Haweswater and Ullswater. The head of Haweswater is encompassed by a grand array of mountains. Away to the west is the long ridge of High Street set on a north-south line, and the route of the Roman road that ran from Carlisle to Ambleside and then westwards to Eskdale and Ravenglass. It is a road that can be seen again at Fell Foot in Little Langdale, in Wrynose Bottom and in Eskdale. No one minds a road with Roman origins, but many deplore the 'irremediable line, a piece of desperate and level slicing gouged across nature's own gradual curves' which Manchester cut along the fell side from the foot of

Haweswater, This was when they raised the level of the lake by ninety feet at the flooding of Mardale. The occasional low level of the lake – in 1973 and 1976 for example – brought many visitors to see the exposed ancient field walls, the rubble of the church, the Dun Bill Inn and the farms of Grove Brae and Goosemire.

Seven miles north-east of Haweswater is Ullswater, extending nine miles from Patterdale to Pooley Bridge. The traveller in search of the 'Picturesque Beauty' of the Lake District, the Revd William Gilpin (1724 – 1804) set out his views on a tour of the Lakes in 1772 – *Observations Relative chiefly to Picturesque Beauty in the Mountains and Lakes of Cumberland and Westmorland.* Ullswater, he wrote, in form 'resembles a Z, only there is no angular acuteness'. The head of the lake at Patterdale is situated amid dramatic scenery, with a fine lake-side walk from Howtown on the eastern bank. It provides views that drew from Gilpin the observation that, 'as we decended a little further, the whole of the lake opened before us, and such a scene as almost drew from us the apostrophe of the enraptured bard : *Visions of glory, spare my aching sight'.*

Wordsworth, who visited Ullswater many times, records one particular visit in November 1805 in his *Guide to the Lakes,* and comments on the small lake of Brothers-water 'named in old ways Broaderwater, and probably rightly so, . . . but the change in the appellation of this small lake or pool (if it be a corruption) may have been assisted by some melancholy accident similar to what happened about twenty years ago when two brothers were drowned there, having gone out to take their holiday pleasure upon the ice on a New-Year's day'. Whilst on his 1805 visit Wordsworth heard of the victory at Trafalgar and the death of Lord Nelson.

In 1878 J. Priestman Atkinson, following a long and distinguished line of compilers of guide-books to the Lake District, issued his *A Week at the Lakes.* Something of what he had to say, and the way it was all depicted, was both prophetic and novel, and his readers were able to follow the adventures of two elegantly-clad strip cartoon figures, Dobbs and Potts.

'Now where shall we go ?' said Potts.

'Let's go to Switzerland, this sort of thing' said Potts, climbing, mountaineer-like on to a chair and table, with a broom-stick held high. After debating on Paris, Potts, demonstrating an agile high can-can kick the meanwhile, the two travellers determined finally to go to the English Lakes, for as Dobbs said : 'Let us see them before they are all turned into reservoirs'.

The rumours of that time of Manchester's interest in extracting water from Thirlmere and from Ullswater were abroad. The aged Ruskin wrote that 'Manchester is plotting to steal the waters of Thirlmere and the clouds of Helvellyn'. It all came true in part, but in the case of Ullswater extraction of water from the lake, now effected by an underground pumping station, is at least unobtrusive. It is also a scene which, ignoring the summer rash of cars on the west shore road of Ullswater, has remained little changed since the poet Thomas Grey visited it in 1769. His *Journal to the Lakes* has many evocative descriptions. He found Ullswater 'opening directly at my feet, majestic in its calmness, clear and smooth as a blue mirror, with winding shores and low points of land covered with green inclosures, white farm houses looking out among the trees, and cattle feeding'.

Whilst it is possible to set out biological definitions of lakes and tarns the variation accepted most commonly is one of size. Devoke Water is admittedly hardly different in area from the undoubted lakes of Loweswater and Brotherswater, but most tarns are very small, set in peaty or rocky ground, and with a margin of reeds and grasses nodding and fluttering in the wind.

Blea Tarn in the upper reaches of the two Langdales, and Red Tarn on Helvellyn attracted Wordsworth's attention : the former in *The Excursion* as 'a liquid pool that glittered in the sun'. The water of Tarn Hows is one of the most visited of all Lake District spots. Lonely and tranquil with only an occasional skater on a deep winter's Monday, it then still bears the scar marks of thousands of summer feet around its lovely tree-fringed lines. From Tarn Hows there is a dramatic view into Langdale and this perhaps brings too may visitors for comfort and for the effective conservation of the area. The tarns scatter the maps like so many blue droplets — seeking the more remote of them is an enriching experience which the poets well knew.

Wordsworth is explicit on tarns. He says of mountain tarns that they are an acceptable sight to the wanderer, not merely as an incident that diversifies the prospect, but as forming in his mind a centre or conspicuous point . . . with water black and sullen'. He was fond of Loughrigg Tarn, near Grasmere, with 'its margin of green firm meadows, of rocks, and rocky woods, a few reeds here, a little company of water-lilies there, with beds of gravel or stone beyond; a tiny stream issuing neither briskly nor sluggishly out of it'.

In such tranquil spots, where John Keats admired 'the tone, the colouring, the slate, the stone, the moss, the rock-wood, or if I may say so, the intellect, the countenance of such places' it is easy to think that 'Industry' never ventured. But the growing interest shown by industrial archaeologists has charted a dimension in Lake District artefacts of considerable size and importance. The early iron industry, those which were powered by water, the coal and iron mining, the quarries, and the woodland industries were the most important, but there was a great variety of minor trades.

J. D. Marshall and Michael Davies-Shiel in their classic, *Industrial Archaeology of the Lake Counties* (1969 and 1977) say: 'it is no exaggeration to say that the mountains of the Lake District are, in places, honeycombed with mineworkings'. Most were for lead and copper, and in the Red Dell valley at Coniston the Company of Mines Royal (who had been active in the Lake District since 1564), mined for copper from about 1599. Most of the traces of such activity which survive are however those made in the nineteenth century.

Among the most impressive are the lead mine workings at Greenside in the Glenridding valley, north of Patterdale, which were not dismantled until 1962 at the mine's closure. The galena ore, yielding 80 per cent of lead and 12oz of silver per ton was mined extensively to an annual output of over 1,000 tons. The demand for water power at Greenside even led to the enlarging of 'Wordsworth's Red Tarn' on Helvellyn.

The quarries provided roofing slates and raw materials for walls and roads. A slate quarry had become established as early as 1283, and was an important trade by the late seventeenth century. The green slate of Borrowdale and Honister belongs to the Borrowdale Volcanic Series with the green colour resulting from a ferrous oxide content. Other quarries at Kirkby-in-Furness (now known as the Burlington Quarries) produce a dark blue slate of Silurian origins. The extension of the railways in the later nineteenth century helped the growth of the quarry trade — slate from Honister had to be sent previously by packhorse some fifteen miles to Ravenglass — and they also brought many more visitors, and business men, to make day-trips and to live in the Lake District. The great Tilberthwaite — Hodge Close quarry worked some three million cubic yards of rock on its green slate working site alone.

The Lake District woodlands thriving up to about the 1,800ft line were well worked by charcoal burners, and a variety of wood-using industries. Tanners, hoopers, coopers, basket-makers, brush-makers, and the wood-turners making bobbins for the Lancashire cotton mills all needed wood for their survival. A large Stockport cotton mill in 1843 was using ten million bobbins at any one time. The industry has left many bobbin-mills including the careful preservation of the Stott Park Bobbin Mill at Finsthwaite, which was fed by water-power from High Dam tarn.

One of the most important Lake District industries from the 1760s onwards was the manufacture of 'gunpowder' in the form of a black blasting powder. At Elterwater and Lowwood the sites of manufacture can still be seen. Charcoal obtained from burning juniper, silver-birch, or alder was mixed with saltpetre and sulphur, and then ground and mixed evenly. The resulting powder was supplied to quarries, iron mines (including many ore extracting mines abroad), railways, for firework manufacture, and for sporting and military use. The combined works employed about 500 adults in the second half of the nineteenth century.

The water-powered mills also housed an active woollen, cotton, flax and silk industry which grew up in the Lake District. Extensive sheep-farming had been carried on since early medieval times by the monastic house at Furness and, using Pennine wool, by those set in the Yorkshire dales. A coarse woollen cloth made Kendal famous by the reign of the first Queen Elizabeth, and the dyed 'Kendal Green' was mentioned by Shakespeare. Finally Kendal has a considerable part still in the provision of snuff, ground from the tobacco which, in the nineteenth century, was imported through the coastal port of Whitehaven.

We have seen that water-power and the spread of the railways had important effects on the growth of Lake District communities. The natural wonders which had brought early northwards *The Lakers* — the title of a superbly written book by the Millom poet, Norman Nicholson — were by the middle years of Queen Victoria's reign open to many. A writer in the *Westmorland Gazette* on April 24, 1847, said, that as Chairman at the inaugural meeting of the Windermere railway line he had :

'come that morning from the other side of Manchester, after breakfasting at an ordinary breakfast time, and he had had the pleasure of taking luncheon at an ordinary time on the banks of Windermere'.

He expected that many a merchant or manufacturer would be likewise carried by express train to 'the shore of that beautiful lake' returning the next morning to the cotton exchange at Manchester or the shipping houses of Liverpool. Such attention brought the erection of many a country villa which became the place which gave to the owner and his family a status, sense of identity and achievement, and in the novels of Jane Austen at least, a permanence.

In arriving at this mid-nineteenth century stage houses in the Lake District were descended from a long succession of variations in building type. The first efforts were those which built castles for defence in the north and in Scotland. It was a natural process for the keep or pele-tower to become an isolated feature, to which a hall range was added.

The domestic architecture of the Elizabethan period in Cumbria again is often a development of a prominent keep with attached buildings. The seventeenth century builders, who created many an attractive farm house, also set out a few houses with classical and baroque overtones. The redoubtable Lady Anne Clifford also rebuilt medieval castles at Appleby, Brougham, Brough, and elsewhere on the borders with Yorkshire such as Skipton Castle.

Whilst the eighteenth century architectural movements had little direct effect in the Lake District — although the delightful circular house of 1774 by John Plaw for Henry Curwen on Belle Isle in Windermere is a notable exception — we have noted also the nineteenth century preoccupation around Windermere. When M. W. Taylor wrote his *Manorial Halls of Westmorland and Cumberland* in 1892 it was perhaps typical of the parson-researching age of the time that he ignored those houses around Windermere completely. No-one was more ardent in his opposition to hordes of visitors brought by the hated railway than Wordsworth, but he was also joined by other fashionable Lakes residents, Lady Fleming, Bishop Watson, Baron de Sternberg, Mrs Bolton of Storrs and others.

At Ullock's Royal Hotel at Bowness the starched tablecloths were regularly laden to accommodate the great parties of what the proprietor, William Bownass, said in 1855 was the patronage of 'receiving within a few years the late Queen Dowager (Adelaide), the King of Saxony, the Prince of Prussia, the Grand Duke Constantine of Russia and most of the principal English and Foreign Families of distinction visiting this romantic and interesting district'. On the one hand Bownass was glad to see the great coach retinues but on the other he was in opposition to the new steam boats on the Lake – there are now modern diesel 'steamers' on both Windermere and Ullswater – which took a rowdier populace within eyeing distance of his elegant establishment.

Towards the Ambleside end of Windermere then, as now there was the Low Wood Hotel, an eighteenth century coaching inn used by the Lake poets. While the lakes lacked the therapeutic healing springs of the spas such as Bath or Leamington, visitors had developed their own pattern of visiting and looking, for the sake of grandeur and to lift up one's eyes to the hills. Miss Harriet Martineau, who settled at Ambleside in 1843, wrote her own *Guide to Windermere* for, as she said:

'A few years ago there was only one meaning to Windermere. It then meant a lake lying among mountains, and so secluded that it was some distinction even for a travelled man to have seen it. Now there is a Windermere Railway Station, and a Windermere post office and hotel . . . This implies that a great many people come to the spot; and the spot is so changed by their coming . . .'

It is a phrase which introduces the final task of assessing the more recent growth of amenities in the Lake District, its great importance as a well-used tourist area, and the attempts to conserve it from over-use and abuse. In Miss Martineau's day, as now, there was a desire to seek 'refreshment of spirit in the beauty and grandeur of its incomparable countryside, and of body in its pure air'.

This was a theme with roots in the eighteenth century. It became more dominant as the increase in the growth of towns and of continuing industrial expansion sent people further afield for green open spaces. With this growth came, sometimes reluctantly and born of pressure by amenity bodies and articulate individuals, legislation designed to protect free access to the countryside. The Commons, Open Spaces and Footpaths Preservation Society was founded in 1865, and the National Trust in 1895, with Canon H. D. Rawnsley of Keswick, an ardent conservationist, as one of its founders. The Trust acquired land near Derwentwater and Ullswater in 1902 and 1906 and is now one of the largest and most efficient landowners in the Lake District.

The 1920s saw the formation of many other amenity bodies such as the Council for the Preservation of Rural England (1926), the influential Friends of the Lake District (1934), and those primarily concerned with free access such as the Youth Hostels Association (1931) and the Ramblers' Association (1935). From 1929 several committees – Addison, Dower and Hobhouse among them – were set up to consider the desirability of following the long lead of America with the setting-up of National Parks. They were finally inaugurated by the 1949 National Parks and Access to the Countryside Act. John Dower in his far-sighted report of 1945 had defined a national park as:

'an extensive area of beautiful and relatively wild country in which, for the nation's benefit and by appropriate national decision and action (a) the characteristic landscape beauty is strictly preserved (b) access and facilities for public open air enjoyment are amply provided (c) wild life and buildings and places of architectural and historic interest are suitably protected while (d) established farming use is effectively maintained'.

It is a statement which has not been superseded but the continuing and changing pressures on national parks led to the 'Sandford Report' of the National Park Policies Review Committee in 1974. However some of its recommendations have been dis- 13 regarded by ministerial decisions within areas of high quality mineral wealth such as the Peak District National Park. In Lakeland the 'Friends of the Lake District' maintain unceasing vigil, but the widening and extension of the A66 road within the National Park was again a battle won by other interests. It did not satisfy the Sandford criterion of being done 'only in the case of a most compelling national necessity'. And no one feels it will be the last case for concern.

In the Lake District – designated a National Park in 1951 – decisions were made and implemented as they affected the statutory charge by the Lake District Planning Board. This was succeeded, at local government reorganisation on April 1, 1974 by the Lake District Special Planning Board consisting of eighteen members appointed by Cumbria County Council and nine members by the Secretary of State for the Environment and serviced by a National Park Officer and his staff. The 'unique combination of spectacular mountains and rugged fells penetrated by pastoral valleys and mirrored in numerous tarns and lakes' within its care includes with it 'all the planning functions which would otherwise be undertaken by the County Council, or the four District Councils' of Allerdale, Copeland, Eden and South Lakeland.

One of the inevitable pressures on an area of great natural beauty, now made more accessible by the north-south motorway, M6, at its eastern edge, is that from tourists and recreational uses. An August traffic survey of 1938/9, contrasted with one for 1975, shows the A591 road from Windermere to Keswick carrying 10 times more vehicles in a 16 hour day. The 12 largest caravan sites now accommodate over 2,500 caravans contrasted to the 1952 total capacity of all sites at 600; it has been necessary to create, and constantly review the need for more, car-parks, especially in the Langdale valleys. 'Focal points such as Tarn Hows receive some half a million visitors a year and several hundred people a day reach the summit of a popular mountain like Helvellyn'. It is activity which has brought forward clearly the basic truth – 'that the public's enjoyment of the Lake District can easily conflict with the conservation of its essential qualities'. The peace, quiet and remoteness is assailed by those most active in seeking it out.

The Lake District Special Planning Board, guided by its then Chief Officer, Kenneth Himsworth, CBE, has set out, with considerable skill and attention to detail, its consideration of all the problems within its area in a *Draft National Park Plan* (1977). After consideration of comments received, the modified draft will be written into the form of the adopted Plan. This will be again reviewed at a period of not longer than five years. The Board's main work is concentrated under the headings of land management, conservation, access and recreation, local people, management services, information and interpretation, its properties, and detailed plans which bring together many aspects of a problem.

It is inevitable that in the busiest valleys and passes traffic management in the forms of one-way schemes, limiting the numbers of vehicles entering the valley head, and more encouragement to leave the car in a 'positive parking area' will be needed. The popular sports of motor-boating and water-skiing have already had speed limits imposed at Coniston Water, Derwentwater, and in due course at Ullswater. But by contrast to what many feel to be inevitable pressures which need control there is a concern to administer so that more access and picnic areas can be developed and car parking management be effectively maintained. The interpretation of all that is to be seen and enjoyed by visitors can best be undertaken at the National Park Information Centre, set in 30 acres a few miles north of Windermere, at Brockhole, or at one of the four other smaller interpretation centres, or five mobile units. The displays, lectures, publications and short courses at Brockhole, not to mention the coffee and short-bread in its cafe attract some 180,000 visitors a year, including at least 30,000 coming in organised educational and youth groups. It is an impressive achievement of lasting value.

There is a peak demand for facilities and recreation which seems to lengthen and

diversify each year, and cause ever-greater volumes of traffic. No organisation can or should attempt to sacrifice all that is worth seeing or doing to such pressure. All that can be done is to maintain acceptable levels and in some cases to reduce demand through management schemes – touring by car and caravan is a pressure causing considerable concern as it can adversely affect the character of the National Park. 'Complete preservation' is however neither possible nor necessarily desirable and sensible compromise is sought constantly.

Let me give here some words by Norman Nicholson. Writing in the excellent guidebook to the Lake District National Park, first published in 1969, he gave this advice :

'To see the Lakes clearly, however, we must pass beyond the photograph or picture ; we must penetrate to the living landscape behind the view. We must get out of our cars, feel the rock under out feet, breathe the Cumbrian air, and learn to know something, at least, of the complex organic life of grass, herb and tree, something of the changing pattern of weather, water and rock, and something of the way man has helped to shape the landscape in the past and is shaping it today. In fact, if we really want to look at the world around us, we must learn to use our knowledge, curiosity, reason, imagination, mind and heart and all five senses as well as just our eyesight'.

As you pass the Lake District National Park signs (depicting the silhouette of Wastwater, and the surrounding mountains) set at each main entrance road it is advice worth heeding. Matthew Arnold wrote in his poem, *Resignation:*

*And now, in front, behold outspread*
*Those upper regions we must tread,*
*Mild hollows, and clear heathy swells,*
*The cheerful silence of the fells.*

The charge to the present is to save and enhance the qualities of the English Lakes for a distant future in which there is no reason to assume that there will not be those who will also care about a unique gift of matchless grandeur.

The illustrations have been arranged in an order based on a visitor first moving northwards from Windermere to Ambleside, and out in a succession of visits through the western valleys. The Lakes of Derwentwater and Ullswater (see pages 74–96) are then best visited from Keswick and Pooley Bridge.

*Geoffrey Beard*

Those who think nostalgically the year round about the Lake District have in mind some such picture as this view of Lake Windermere, taken near Waterhead at the head of the lake. Hills, water, boats, rolling clouds and thickly wooded bays and promontories assail the mind and eye. Lake Windermere, over ten miles long, is the largest in England and has become the busiest. From the late 19th century it has been the setting for regattas and water-spectacles, and four passenger boats (see page 18) ply its length from spring to autumn. If memory will be selective for a moment and exclude the boats and house, the Lake, with the backdrop of Bowfell and the Langdale Pikes, must look almost as it did when Roman legionaries settled at 'Galava', near Ambleside.

16

At the southern end of Lake Windermere a road on the eastern side climbs away high at Gummer's How to afford spectacular views. The Lake 'steamers' (actually diesel-driven) are moored near the terminus of the Lakeside Railway – now run by steam enthusiasts (see page 110). The rich hardwood slopes gave fuel for the charcoal smelting of iron-ore by the Romans. With no villages on the western shore, and with houses well hidden, it is still possible to walk near the shore for many miles, with fine distant views as inspiration, and only, at times, water-fowl for company.

At this southern end of the Lake the National Trust have established Fell Foot Country Park which provides chalet accommodation, caravan sites, boating, swimming and an attractive restaurant.

Troutbeck lies to the east of the road from Windermere to Ambleside (A591) and amongst its many farms is that of 'Townend', dating from about 1626. Now owned by the National Trust, and open to the public, the house was originally occupied from the 17th century until 1944 by successive generations of the Brownes, yeoman farmers. It is furnished with their oak furniture and other possessions.

The house, which has many characteristic features in the local tradition, such as the cylindrical chimneys, is divided into two sections for 'living' and 'working'. There are later additions and variations in the shapes and types of windows, but these do little to impair an interesting home, carefully preserved, but an all-too-rare survival of a past age.

20

Ambleside has many swirling becks and rivers and a fine waterfall, Stock Ghyll Force. The abundance of water-power saw the rise of many fulling and bobbin mills. This wheel worked a corn mill, and has been recently reinstated to work its magic spell on curious visitors. It is an 'overshot' wheel revolving against the current flowing past its base, and is some 18ft in diameter. High maintenance costs and changes in usage have ensured that many wheels have been neglected – their importance to former Lakeland industries in a pre-steam age was incalculable.

22

Lakeland is perhaps at its finest in the autumn, a viewpoint endorsed by William Wordsworth in his *Guide to the Lakes* (5th edn 1835) — 'the months of September and October (particularly October) are generally attended with much finer weather; and the scenery is then, beyond comparison, more diversified, more splendid, and beautiful . . .'.

One of Wordsworth's favourite viewpoints lay at the eastern end of Rydal Water, seen here with the early touch of 'splendid beautiful' autumn upon it. The lake is small, some two miles north-west of Ambleside, and with the busy road to Keswick (A591) skirting its eastern shore, visitors soon find the lakeside path on the western side, towards Loughrigg Terrace. It has become one of the most used in the Lake District, in scenery, 'beyond comparison'.

24

South-west of Grasmere the Langdale valley, with its narrow stone-walled roads, affords many views on the way to the small village of Chapel Stile. This view shows Grasmere in the middle distance with its lake, surrounded by land owned by the National Trust, and the Lake District Special Planning Board of the National Park.

A favourite route to the summit of Helvellyn is from Grasmere following the old pack-horse tracks north of Grisedale Tarn. To the north-west of the village and to the left of this view is Helm Crag, with prominent rocks resembling in shape a lion couchant with a lamb between its paws. Wordsworth, his wife and his daughter lived nearby at Dove Cottage and at their deaths were buried at Grasmere in St Oswald's churchyard.

26

Park House with its strong stone barn lies below the Ambleside to Coniston road (A593). Behind is the Elterwater valley and the many-peaked mass of Silver Howe. The Lake lies hidden in the trees: it is among the smallest, with some private ownership of its banks.

The village of Elterwater can be seen in the left middle distance and the percipient may find a glimpse of the lake through the trees. A gunpowder mill worked at Elterwater from 1824 to World War I and the site is now a carefully maintained hotel, chalet and caravan enterprise.

The National Trust are the owners of Tarn Hows since its presentation to them in 1930 by the Scott family in memory of Sir James and Lady Scott. It is one of the most frequented spots in the Lake District and the serious erosion of footpaths has led to the dominant but necessary laying of gravel and edging to those around the water, and the provision of nearby car-parks, albeit well hidden by trees.

Lying north-west of Hawkshead, Tarn Hows — the name means 'a small lake' and derives from the Norse word *tjorn* — is backed by the Langdale Pikes, and is itself at a height of 700ft above sea-level.

The autumn colouring is one of the delights
to the eye when visiting the Lake District.
North of Coniston on the Ambleside road
(A593) is this small reed-fringed Yew Tree
Tarn, with Holme Fell in the background. It
was all formerly a moss and was dammed
at the south end in the 1930s by James
Marshall and stocked with fish. Water-fowl
dot the placid dark surface of the tarn. The
public may fish there by application to the
Coniston and Torver Angling Club: a
32   splendid way to relax.

Looking across Coniston Water to the Old Man of Coniston range from the eastern bank at the northern end of the lake is a delight in any season. In late spring with the rhododendrons in bloom, boats bobbing at anchor, and with Coniston village grey and white in the middle distance it is easy to imagine it is at its best. A mile below this viewpoint, on the same eastern bank, is Brantwood, John Ruskin's home for 25 years until he died in 1900. It was on Coniston Water that Donald Campbell attempted to break the water-speed record in 1967 and crashed to his death.

34

Coniston Water, with *Gondola* the oldest
surviving iron boat in the north. This has
been saved from the scrapyard by a local
enthusiast and an appeal has been launched
for £95,000 by the National Trust, who
intend to restore the 85ft boat to its former
glory, and to have it in service again by 1980
on the five mile lake. It has now been re-
moved to land for restoration to begin.

*Gondola* was launched in 1859 by the
Furness Railway Company having been
built for the Duke of Devonshire, President
of that company, and the Duke of Buccleuch
who owned the bed of the lake. It carried
visitors on pleasure trips until World War II.

38

Two miles north of Coniston the road to Ambleside (A593) is joined at its west side by a minor road to High Tilberthwaite where it ends. Further upstream the beck flows in a series of waterfalls deep below precipitous walls of rock. Paths run on both banks and into the heart of the gorge where a view-point bridge has been built. The stream was low when this photograph was taken.

It is always desirable to leave a car at a convenient and sensible spot for this sort of journey and walk by the footpath on the eastern bank. The National Trust has established an adventure hut in a disused quarry nearby, which can accommodate up to ten people — an ideal centre for fell-walking in the Little Langdale valley.

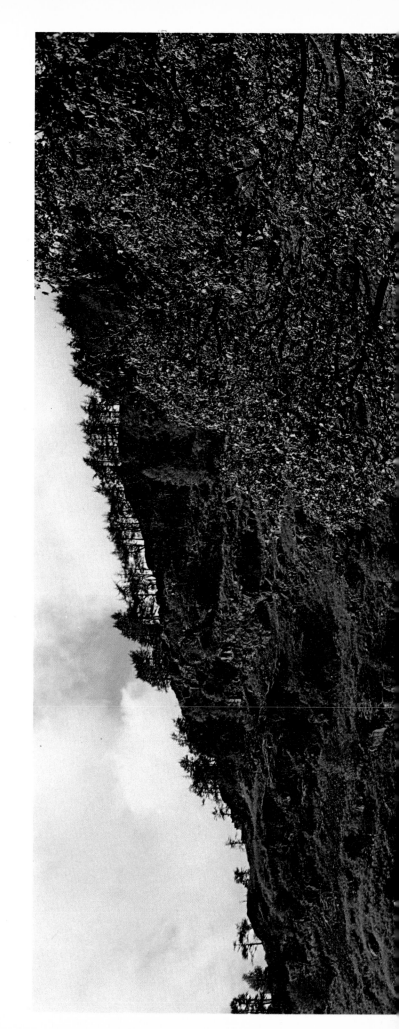

Due south of Hawkshead a minor road runs along the west bank of Esthwaite Water, set amid the low green fields. The area is well farmed, and here, at Esthwaite Hall, the cows gaze at all-comers placidly in fields which run down to the quiet shores of Esthwaite Water. The strong farmhouse with its cylindrical chimney is a splendid example of local traditions in building, which are also seen to advantage in the skilfully made dry-stone wall.

40

The little grey village of Chapel Stile in the Great Langdale valley lies west of Ambleside (B5343) just beyond Elterwater. The houses were mostly built in stone and slate for the workers at the gunpowder mill (see page 28). The church, Holy Trinity, dates from 1857. The dramatic environs are owned by the National Trust who have done much in the Lake District to facilitate public access, subject to the needs of agriculture, forestry and nature conservation. Beautiful green slate is still quarried in this area.

42

The road from Ambleside out through Chapel Stile (B5543) continues into Great Langdale. At Dungeon Ghyll the waterfall of Stickle Gill (see page 46) drops dramatically from Stickle Tarn. The Tarn lies hidden below Pavey Ark (2,288ft), the rocky face of which just rises above the bracken slopes on the right. The higher peak is Harrison Stickle. The dark rocky nob of nearby Pike How is a rewarding viewpoint.

The draft plan prepared by the special Planning Board for the Lake District National Park (1977) says: 'rock-climbing is a fast-growing activity and at times the more accessible faces in Borrowdale and Langdale are thronged with climbers'. In the vicinity of Stickle Gill, 1,400ft up on a summer's day one knows that to be true.

Stickle Gill waterfalls near Dungeon Ghyll (see page 44) in the Great Langdale valley, often called Mill Gill as the rushing waters were in times past so used at the foot. The waterfalls reflect rapidly the preceding weather; sometimes after heavy storms, not infrequent in Langdale, becoming a tremendous torrent.

It is a final climb for only well-equipped walkers who then carry on up the less forbidding side of the Langdale Pikes, subsiding exhausted and triumphant. It is necessary to be ever-mindful of weather and sensible precautions for the return descent. The final peak should only be attempted by properly equipped walkers.

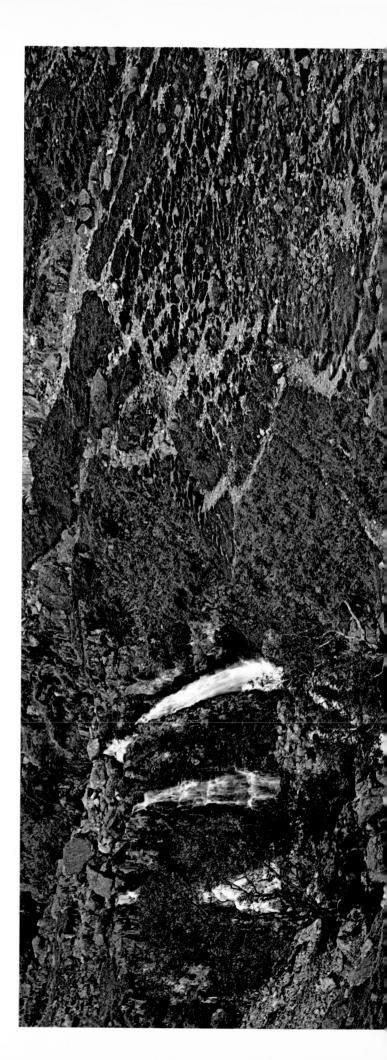

South of the road (B5543) at Dungeon Ghyll is the best known of the several Blea Tarns in the Lake District. In his 'Guide to the Lakes' Wordsworth refers to his description of the Tarn in his poem *The Excursion*. It has been a popular spot since the late 18th century with a fine view of the Langdale Pikes away to the north-west. Wordsworth's 'liquid pool that glittered in the sun' was then in 'a quiet treeless nook', but later plantings of trees and rhododendrons have given a colourful edge where perhaps none is needed.

48

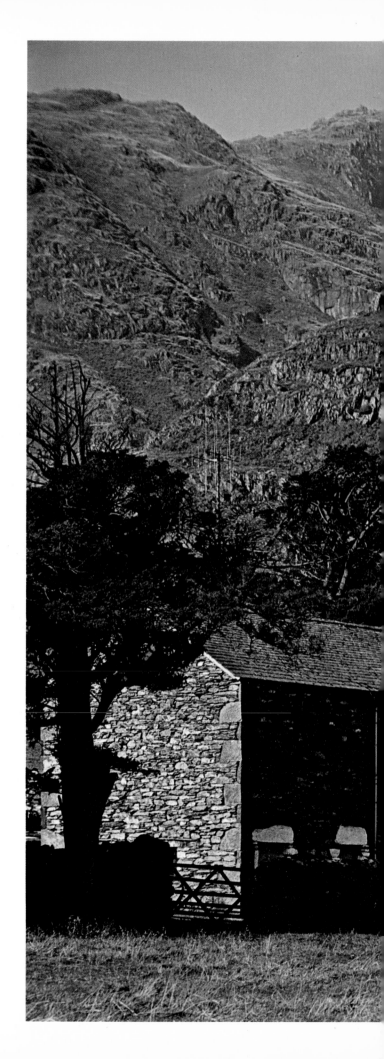

At the bottom of the Wrynose Pass in Little Langdale this farm, named like so many other buildings and places in the Lake District, Fell Foot, is another National Trust property. Behind it rises the precipitous slopes of Blake Rigg, an outlier of Pike o'Blisco. These central fells, composed of Borrowdale Volcanic rocks, give rise to dramatic scenery.

50

Since the days of the Romans, who journey-
ed between their forts at Galava (at
Ambleside) and Hardknott, the narrow
precipitous road through the Wrynose and
Hard Knott Passes has always been busy.
The River Duddon is crossed by this bridge
near Cockley Beck. The peak in the background is Harter Fell, a shapely mountain
which lies between Eskdale and Dunner-
dale. The road congestion and 'the attraction of the road as a motoring experience',
high, dramatic and dangerous, means that
it will be necessary to maintain low traffic
volume if these areas are to retain their
character. Despite the unsuitability of the
passes for cars towing caravans some still
try. It is an all-too-frequent planners'
dilemma with spectacular scenery the
hostage for too many.

'The Friends of the Lake District' have always encouraged those who maintain the traditional stone-walls and hedges in the National Park. This good example built in pink granite can be seen in Eskdale on the Hard Knott Pass road near Brotherikeld, a little west of the Roman fort. The upper reaches of the Esk, to be explored only on foot, are in the heart of the mountains and remain wild and lonely.

The conical peak in the right background is Bowfell (2,960ft), a mountain which dominates also the head of Langdale and Langstrath, a branch of Borrowdale. The summit of Bowfell is a mass of shattered rock and very rugged.

54

Some 2½ miles SW of the foot of Coniston Water the Ulverston to Broughton-in-Furness road (A5092) affords this spectacular view from Wood Gate north towards Torver High Common and Coniston Old Man in the centre distance. To its left is Dow Crag, well known to rock climbers. In the middle distance, bracken covered, is Beacon Fell, a marvellous viewpoint, and easily attainable, only entailing a walk of a little more than a mile. The land over Subberthwaite seen in the foreground is pastoral and within the 1,200ft contour levels. From Broughton-in-Furness the A593 runs north-east in a dramatic valley to Torver and then along the western side of Coniston Water back to Ambleside.

Wast Water in west Lakeland is best reached either by the dramatic Wrynose and Hard Knott passes from Ambleside or from the coastal road running north to Whitehaven (A595). Ringed by mountainous country — Great Gable (see page 60) is but 2 miles to the north-east. Visitors never cease to be amazed at the loose rock screes of the Borrowdale volcanics which, dark and menacing, shoot right down to the very deep lake bed as they have done from the remote Ice Age.

At Wasdale Head splendid views are afforded of the high fells and down the length of the lake. Most of this is National Trust land — concealed camp sites, a youth hostel at former Wasdale Hall, and good walking in Copeland Forest make it attractive to many, but with ingenuity solitude can be found.

On the western shore near the head of Wast Water with Great Gable (in the centre background) rising to 2,950ft. The water in the lake, like that of Ennerdale, is very pure, and comparatively few plants and animals live therein because of the shortage of nutrients.

Since Neolithic times farming communities have managed to penetrate the hillier ground beyond the main settlements. One of the small modern hill farms can be seen at the left centre, with pasture-land pushing the golden gorse back to the water's edge.

Five miles inland from Windscale near Calder Bridge on the Cumbrian coast road (A595) are the ruins of Calder Abbey, a Cistercian house founded in 1134. The view here shows the five arches of the north transept and part of the eastern tower. As a daughter house to Furness Abbey Calder had a troublous history in Scottish raids, causing the monks to leave and settle at Byland in Yorkshire. Calder suffered the fate of most monasteries at the Dissolution in 1536 and has declined slowly into a gracious ruin. The chancel contains the stone effigies of three 13th century knights in chain mail.

Twelve miles north-east of Whitehaven at the foot of the Loriton valley is the small lake of Lowes Water. This view is taken from the minor road at the eastern end of the lake looking towards the undulating hills of Lowes Water Fell. Fishing rights on the lake are owned by the National Trust, and when the heather is out few finer settings can be found for a day's sport. A mile or so to the south-east lies Crummock Water (see page 66) into which Lowes Water flows. This area is best explored from Cockermouth, six miles to the north, or on a dramatic day's motoring from Keswick, over the Honister Pass to see Buttermere, Crummock Water and Lowes Water. However some further restriction on traffic using Honister Pass is a desirable trend.

64

Crummock Water lies a little to the south-east of Lowes Water (see page 64) and the winding minor road from Cockermouth (B5289) runs along its eastern bank. The southern hills of Lowes Water Fell run along the western and southern banks, and are part of the Skiddaw Slate series. This gives a softer outline than the sharp rocks of the Borrowdale volcanics (see page 50). Again the land is owned by the National Trust, affording access on foot to the lake at several points. A mile or two to the south-east is Buttermere (see page 68).

Buttermere is the favourite small lake with many Lake District visitors, and here, in its autumn colouring, with evening light dappling leaves and the water it is easy to see why. The road on its north-east side continues through the small village of Buttermere to the south and on to the Honister Pass (see page 70) and Borrowdale. Most of the land and the lake is owned by the National Trust, but the very considerable impact of vehicles on Buttermere village, the commons and the lake shore is causing the National Park authorities to consider early remedial measures — restrictions on coaches, a valley bus service, and 'positive' parking areas.

68

A co-ordinated traffic policy in the National Park — the subject of long debate — seems the more urgent when one travels over the dramatic winding Honister Pass with, in this picture, the dark mass of Honister Crag dominant on the left, and the lower slopes of Hindsgarth to the right. The effect of one unsuitable vehicle on the climb from 300 to near 1,200ft may be imagined and is still all too frequently encountered. The access to beautiful scenery, with, at the western end the lakes of Buttermere, Crummock Water and Lowes Water is the obvious attraction.

Honister slate is still quarried, now from near the summit of the Crag. It has been worked since the mid-18th century, for many years from the precipitous face of the Crag, reached only by tracks which still cling perilously to the steep sides.

In the lower western reaches of the Honister Pass the road passes and crosses the Gatesgarthdale Beck, which drains into Buttermere. It looks swift and clean but contains a great deal of slate dust from the Honister quarries. One of the problems of slate quarrying is the considerable accumulation of waste material — 'as much as 95% of the quarried rock becomes waste material'. However the employment benefits have to be measured carefully by the National Park authorities alongside the damage to the landscape.

72

No photographic survey of the Lake District can ever exclude Ashness Bridge with Derwent Water and the interlacing cones of the Skiddaw massif in the background.

The strong stone arch fits so well into the landscape. It carries the narrow twisting road to Watendlath, running through oak woodlands into a seemingly remote valley before the little hamlet, made famous by Sir Hugh Walpole's novels, is reached.

Another view near Ashness Bridge (see page 74) at the south-east end of Derwent Water. Within four miles of Keswick it can be seen in this view how quickly the small towns of the Lake District are left behind for bracken fells and tumbling rocky waters. The geological formation here is of the Skiddaw Slate series formed 500 to 450 million years ago. Where the rock has broken down into small beds of soil, bracken and heather flourish, and the outlines of the hills are softer and less angular.

Sunset over Derwent Water and Bassenthwaite Lake taken from 'Surprise View' near to Ashness Bridge (see pages 74–76). From this vantage point one sees the length of Derwent Water and to the western fells and the foot of Bassenthwaite Lake. Derwent Water has many small islands dotted across its surface. A recent decision by the Home Secretary has restricted the power boat speed on this beautiful lake, and on Coniston Water (see page 34) to 10mph.

78

View over Glencoyne Park from the western bank of Ullswater below where the A5091 to Matterdale leaves the lakeside road (A592). A similar restriction on power boat speeds on Ullswater to those on Derwent Water and Coniston Water will come into effect in 1983. Ullswater is a busy lake with difficult parking problems for cars alongside its western bank, but the area is unbeaten for what the 'Friends of the Lake District' organisation typifies as 'quiet recreation'; walking, fishing, climbing, sailing, picnicking, or just admiring the scenery.

Water is abstracted from Ullswater by pumping into Haweswater by the North West Water Authority, then flowing by gravity some 90 miles to Manchester and other Lancashire towns. No evidence of the use of this lake for water supply is to be seen; the pumping machinery is underground and the lake is never drawn down.

A little way up the Matterdale road (A5091) on the western bank of Ullswater is Aira Force, the scene of Wordsworth's *The Somnambulist*. The wooded ravine of Aira Beck brings the visitor to the two viewpoint bridges of the Force, which is best seen after heavy rain. On the lake shore at Aira Point are the fields which inspired Wordsworth to write of:

*A host of golden daffodils,*
*Beside the lake, beneath the trees.*
*Fluttering and dancing in the breeze.*

They are, alas, too often dug up by visitors, to be ever replaced by the long-suffering National Trust.

82

Ullswater near Glencoyne Bridge, on the western bank road from Pooley Bridge (A592), south to Glenridding. A splendid group of farm buildings, Lake District vernacular grouping at its best, nestles at the foot of wooded Glencoyne Brow.

A fine way to see Ullswater is to use the passenger 'steamer' which sails the length of the lake from Glenridding to Pooley Bridge, calling at Howtown. Even more rewarding is the walk from Howtown to Patterdale by the lovely east shore path, taking the 'steamer' one way.

A possibility of rain as storm clouds darken over Ullswater at Glencoyne Wood, a property of the National Trust. The road from the Kirkstone Pass and Patterdale to Penrith runs along this shore, giving wide views across Ullswater's ever-changing surface to Hallin and Place Fells. It is as beautiful a road as any in the Lake District and has remained almost unchanged, winding its way between the tiny hamlets, through the woodland, beneath the splendid beeches of Glencoyne, by rocky shore and pebbly beaches. Here the intent fisherman is seen and the white-sailed dinghies are driven before fitful winds.

86

From Patterdale at the southern head of Ullswater it is possible to take public paths on to the eastern slopes of Patterdale Common above the lake. The quiet and intricate complex of valleys which make up Martindale provide a wealth of attractive scenes. Here at Boardalehead in the evening light the bracken is 'ablaze' and the low light emphasises the structure of the land. One can walk on good tracks over Boardale Hause to Patterdale or, more strenuously, take the Ullswater lake shore path and encircle Place Fell.

In a south-westerly direction from the southern end of Ullswater the Grisedale Beck flows away under Grisedale Bridge some 12½ miles to Grisedale Tarn. In the autumn it is flanked by richly coloured trees and misty folded hills. The Mountain Rescue posts which are marked on the map however are indications that care should always be taken to observe both the Country Code, and to take sensible decisions backed by the right clothing and equipment. Even in late summer bracken can be waist-high and hide a fallen walker.

A popular route to Helvellyn runs across the far slopes to go by the rocky ridge of Striding Edge to the summit. This is a route not to be taken lightly, for it can, in bad weather and high winds, become as dangerous as any path in the Lake District.

90

This is the farm Wintercrag in Martindale
standing close to Christy Bridge over the
Hawegarth Beck. A few hundred yards
away is the old chapel built in 1633 on the
site of a much more ancient church. It is
starkly simple in its siting and its interior. It
contains a 14th century holy-water stoup
which has been heavily scored by arrow
sharpening.

This is splendid hill country and the
unclassified road which follows the beck
terminates at Dale Head. A footpath then
climbs over Beda Fell westwards into
Patterdale.

Another view of the Martindale hill country (see page 92) and the Beck, crossed by a foot-bridge. The play of light and shade in these deep valleys is always impressive at every season of the year. From deep green to pale purple the gradations of colour have inspired artists since the late 18th century to attempt watercolour copies. Martindale Common supports a fine herd of red deer owned by the Dalemain estate.

The Martindale valleys are served by only one narrow road which rises from Howtown, steep and twisting, over the Hause. At the top of the Pass it is easy to climb to the summit of Hallin Fell, obtaining extensive views over Ullswater, and also over the Eden Valley as far as the highest Pennines.

Below lie the farms and buildings about the foot of the Hause and the roads to the inner fastnesses of Boardale and Bannerdale. There too is the Vicarage, seen in this picture, the home of the incumbent for the more modern church at the top of the pass.

Haweswater lost some of its natural grandeur in 1929 when Manchester, unable to satisfy its water needs by extraction from Thirlmere, raised the level by construction of a dam. This flooded the little village of Mardale at the valley head. Along the eastern shore an unclassified road runs but this view, across the reservoir, of Haweswater, is taken from Whiteacre Crag, the highest point attained by the road. The wooded peninsula to the left is The Rigg and the remote valley beyond, and to the left, Riggindale, to be reached only on foot. The peak above is Kidsty Pike (2,560ft).

The Lake District is ringed by a number of 'gateway' towns affording access to its rich scenery — Kendal, Ambleside, Keswick and, in the north-east, Penrith. East of Penrith the A66 road passes Brougham Castle, now a popular picnic spot but in the 13th century an important fortification against the Scots. The keep dates from about 1175, but the structure was well repaired in 1651 by Lady Anne Clifford, a remarkable restorer of castles owned by her family.

Brougham lies just below the weir where the Rivers Eamont and Lowther join, and within a few hundred yards of the Roman fort of 'Brocavum' which guarded an important junction of roads.

West of Penrith the A6 road – the old road to Scotland prior to the construction of the motorway (M6) – passes through the high village of Shap. Nearby are the ruins of Shap Abbey founded by the White Canons – the Premonstratensians – in 1199. It was dissolved in the troublous reign of Henry VIII in 1540. After the Dissolution many of its stones were used in the building of the first Lowther Castle, destroyed by fire in 1718. This is moorland pasture country set on the Cumbrian granite fault. In consequence a considerable amount of quarrying goes on for road materials.

The village of Milburn, due east of Penrith, and set in a triangle between the roads to Alston (A686) and Appleby (A66) follows a familiar Cumbrian pattern. As at Askham to the north-west the houses are set around a central green. With its maypole and grazing horses the pattern of village life has undergone little basic change since medieval times. An enclosed village green made it easier to defend against raiders from the north, and in peaceful times to pasture cattle in the winter.

One of the important 'gateway' towns to the Lake District from the east is Appleby, with its sloping Boroughgate running from the Castle to the Church of St Lawrence and the 16th century Moot Hall. In the church are the imposing tombs of Margaret, Countess of Cumberland, and her celebrated daughter, Lady Anne Clifford. Appleby Castle, as Brougham (see page 100) owes much to her careful restoration work.

Appleby, on a loop of the River Eden was the county town of Westmorland until local government reorganisation in 1974. It is the scene of the famous gipsy horse fair each year.

On the south side of Kendal and passed by the old coach road to the north (A6) is Sizergh Castle, still the historic home of the Stricklands, but now administered by the National Trust. Like most important Lake District homes which needed in past times to repel Scottish raiders, Sizergh is built around a massive pele-tower. Domestic quarters were added about 1450 (Great Hall) and in Elizabethan times.

The interior of the house has a 'wealth of early Elizabethan woodwork of high quality': some of that from the Inlaid Room was moved to the Victoria and Albert Museum in 1891. Virginia creeper in autumn colouring has softened the outlines of a notable fortified house, surrounded now by its walled garden.

Since the later 19th century visitors to the Lake District have travelled to the junction of Oxenholme, and on by train or road to Windermere. That line (from London to Glasgow) is now served by 'electric' trains, and the nostalgia of steam is only found, as here, on the Lakeside Railway at the south-west end of Lake Windermere, or on the Ravenglass and Eskdale Railway, south of Whitehaven. It is one way to explore a small area, and fun for adults and children. Most visitors however will want, hopefully, to park their cars carefully in allotted spaces, and in the right clothing and footwear — just walk.

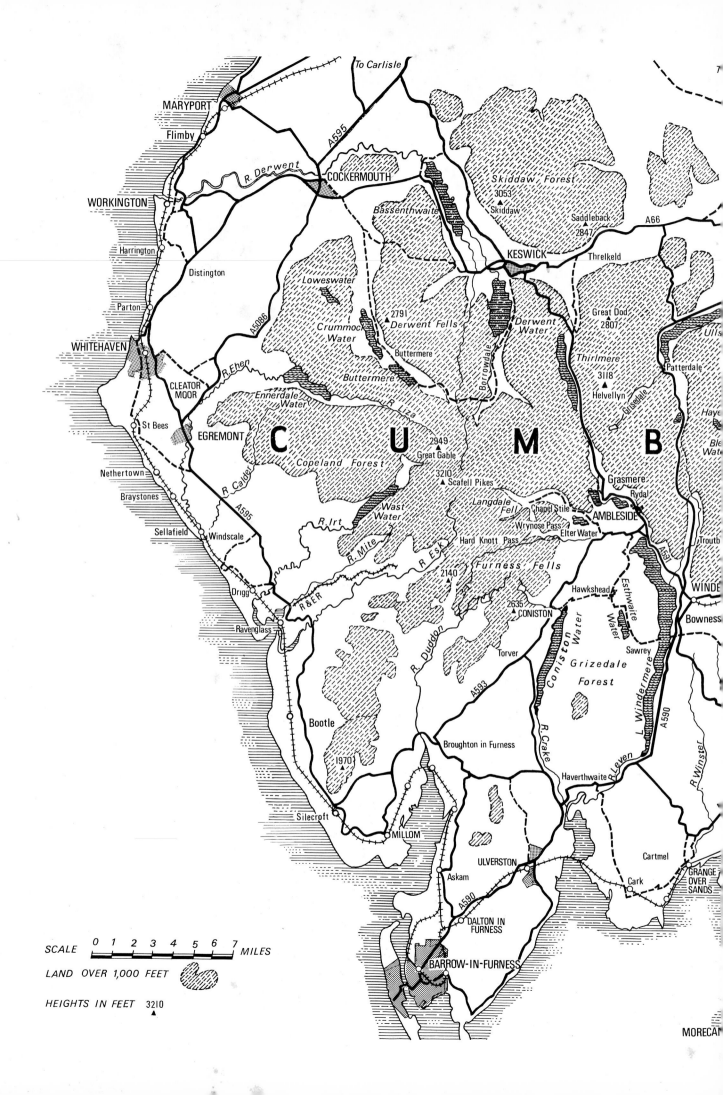

MARYPORT

Flimby

To Carlisle

*R. Derwent*

COCKERMOUTH

WORKINGTON

*Bassenthwaite*

*Skiddaw Forest*

3053
▲ Skiddaw

Saddleback
2847 ▲

A66

Harrington

Distington

*Loweswater*

KESWICK

Threlkeld

Great Dod
2807 ▲

Parton

2791
▲ *Derwent Fells*

*Crummock Water*

Buttermere

*Derwent Water*

*Thirlmere*

3118
▲ Helvellyn

*Grisedale*

Patterdale

Uls

WHITEHAVEN

*R. Ehen*

*Buttermere*

*Borrowdale*

Haye

CLEATOR MOOR

*R. Calder*

*Ennerdale Water*

*R. Liza*

**C U M B**

Ble
Wate

St Bees

A5086

EGREMONT

*Copeland Forest*

2949
Great Gable

Grasmere

Rydal

Nethertown

*R. Calder*

3210
▲ Scafell Pikes

*Langdale Fell*

Chapel Stile

AMBLESIDE

Braystones

A595

*Wast Water*

Wrynose Pass

Elter Water

Troutb

Sellafield

Windscale

*R. Irt*

*R. Mite*

Hard Knott Pass

*R. Esk*

2140
▲

*Furness Fells*

WINDE

Drigg

Hawkshead

*Esthwaite Water*

Bowness

Ravenglass

R & E R

2635
▲ CONISTON

*Coniston Water*

Sawrey

*Grizedale Forest*

L Windermere

A591

Torver

*R. Duddon*

A593

*R. Crake*

Bootle

Broughton in Furness

*R. Leven*

Haverthwaite

A590

*R. Winster*

1970
▲

Silecroft

MILLOM

ULVERSTON

Cartmel

Cark

GRANGE OVER SANDS

Askam

A590

DALTON IN FURNESS

BARROW-IN-FURNESS

MORECA

SCALE  0 1 2 3 4 5 6 7  MILES

LAND OVER 1,000 FEET

HEIGHTS IN FEET  3210
▲